Written for both therapists and patients! A fundamental, healthy relationship primer presented in a short story format with compelling illustrations. Helpful for individual, family, and couples counseling.

Images move and inspire us. A single one may convey a complex or profound concept much more effectively than language alone. Like sound, the visual sense is one of our most important learning tools. Different brain structures are associated with each sense, and the more of the brain we engage, the better we learn.

This illustrated short story may complement the dialogue exchanged during a psychotherapeutic session by providing insight into the dynamics of family and couples relationships. In addition, the images may be reproduced as helpful reminders for clients to take home.

Cartoon Counseling

By Elizabeth R Burchard, LSW

Two Poles Press, Bergenfield, NJ

© 2020, January by Elizabeth R. Burchard, LSW

All rights reserved. No part of this publication may be reproduced or transmitted in any form or by any means, without permission in writing from the author.

Published by Two Poles Press, LLC, Bergenfield, NJ

eISBN 9781576339992

ISBN 9781576339985 (Therapist's Edition 8.5x11)

ISBN 9781576339978 (Client's Edition 5.5x8.5)

Art by Jared Phillips and Howard Bender

Conceptualized by Elizabeth Burchard and Judith Carlone

Cover art by Jared Phillips ©1998

Printed in the United States of America.

Part I

Adam

Examine Yourself

It was another Blue Monday. Adam sat at the edge of the couch, where he had spent the night. He bent over to tie his shoes, but couldn't quite reach the laces. Filled with angst, Adam squeezed his spare tire. Life was not going well. Last month, they had passed him over for a work promotion. The estrangement between him and his wife, Eve, had deepened. In fact, these days they barely spoke. *What am I doing wrong? I want to find out,* Adam pondered.

To be sure, life had dealt Adam his measure of blows, but he had always viewed himself as a survivor, not a victim. *I will find my way. I have overcome obstacles before!*

<-- 3 -->

Stuck

*I*t's time for a tune-up and a reboot! Adam decided to consult a therapist for help.

The therapist, Susan, asked Adam what he hoped to accomplish.

Adam tried to respond, but nothing came. He truly felt suffocated. *I used to have joy and goals. What happened to my passion?*

<-- 5 -->

Susan smiled warmly at Adam. "So, tell me about your concerns."

"My wife, Eve," Adam began hesitantly, "my job, my weight, my brother ..." Then it all burst forth. Adam's thoughts and emotions overwhelmed him in a confused and anxious swarm. "Too, too much," he moaned.

Susan assured him of her support and guidance to tackle his issues. She had plenty of experience.

<-- 6 -->

High Anxiety

Rewire Yourself

Then, she leaned toward Adam and made eye contact. "We can't control everything that happens to us, but we *do* have the power to change our responses. We can work together on reconstruction. How does that sound?"

"I'll give it a try," Adam stated, although his self-confidence left much to be desired.

Susan, however, was upbeat. "So, where shall we begin?"

<-- 9 -->

Enemy Within

Adam scratched his head. "Well … my spare tire, I guess—donuts are my Achilles Heel," he groaned, acknowledging his inner battle. One side championed his greater good, and the other was pleasure seeking, regardless of the consequences. Each morning, he promised himself a donut-free day. Yet, inevitable, subversive thoughts subtly wore down his willpower. His mind, the self-indulgent puppeteer, would escort him down the block toward the local Donut Heaven with specious reassurances. *Today, you deserve a reward. It's OK, you'll do better tomorrow.*

<-- 11 -->

When temptation won yet again, Adam would beat himself up fiercely. He felt weak and worthless. Two inches tall.

Susan suggested that self-condemnation only serves to fuel that destructive, internal force. "Changing a habit is tough for anyone. You might try owning the healthy part—the authentic Adam. He will get you through to the winning side. Assign that unwelcome intruder its own name."

Adam chose "Judas." From that day forward, every time a donut called his name, he would identify Judas as the culprit.

<-- 12 -->

Condemnation

Coach Yourself

Susan then reminded Adam to refrain from negative self-references such as 'failure,' 'hopeless,' and 'lazy,' which only stoke anger and poor esteem. "Encouragement and recognizing your personal strengths motivates empowerment. Remember, you are under construction and every brick you lay counts. Even the smallest!"

Adam resigned himself to the challenge.

"I think this has been a productive session," Susan shared. "How about if you bring your wife to the next one?" Susan wanted to know Eve's perspective.

<-- 15 -->

Part II

Adam
and Eve

Impossible Hug

To the couple standing hesitantly in the doorway, Susan motioned toward the couch. "So where did you two meet?" Susan inquired of Eve once they had settled in.

"In a disco during Spring Break. Our eyes locked across the crowded dance floor and sparks flew."

"We both knew," Adam murmured.

Eve teared up. After 15 years and three children, that former intimacy was hard to find. Yet Eve sensed their love was still alive underneath.

Adam agreed.

<-- 19 -->

Social Demands

Adam sighed. "Keeping up with financial and social obligations is overwhelming. I rarely have a moment to myself."

"The children, the house, that second salary … I'm on autopilot. Numb," Eve added.

<-- 21 -->

Eve continued, "Life was so much simpler when I was growing up, my parents didn't have to establish a college fund before my first birthday, and today's technological necessities had yet to be invented. Now, life feels like an endless struggle, and with all we do, we never seem to get ahead."

<-- 22 -->

Swimming Upstream

Others' Needs

Eve prided herself on being a good parent. Unfortunately, meeting her children's needs left little time for herself or her relationship with Adam.

"It sounds like sometimes, you're last on the list," Susan commented.

Eve nodded in agreement.

<-- 25 -->

Impulsively, Eve turned toward Adam with an intense look. "And I'm last on your list too. You have no time for me. That big noisy screen never takes a rest. You're obsessed with sports. *I'm a football widow.* You should have married that electronic monstrosity instead of me."

Adam shrank lower in his seat and sheepishly glanced away.

Susan reflected, "I can see there are some strong emotions here."

<-- 26 -->

Married to the TV

Eve exclaimed, "Oh, believe me, there's more. *Like your brother, Seth!*"

"Oh? Tell me," Susan probed.

"Seth is a 'prodigy,' self-proclaimed that is. He's living in our basement; no rent in sight, and weekends he monopolizes the garage with his band—'the next Rolling Stones.' He assures us that fame and fortune are just around the corner. When he 'hits it big,' he'll make it up to us. He's a legend in his own mind and his promises are empty. And Adam defends him. 'He's just following his dream,' he says." Eve's tone was angry and mocking.

<-- 28 -->

Self-Absorbed

Pitching Marbles

Eve continued, "Months ago, Seth requested to crash for 'only a few days.' He's overstayed his welcome! To me, he is officially persona non grata."

Eve described repeated attempts to solicit a firm departure date, always skillfully avoided with interruptions, talking over, and strategic subject changes. "He throws me off balance; I can't gain any ground. It's hopeless," Eve sighed.

<-- 31 -->

The Narcissist

Seth's 'higher calling' left no time for gainful employment. Inevitably hurting for cash, he habitually finagled a few bucks from his brother, promptly spent at local clubs where he met with 'important contacts' in the entertainment field.

Susan pointed out that Seth seemed to feel entitled to their unconditional hospitality without gratitude or reciprocation.

Eve agreed. "He's unappreciative, and he's never wrong."

Adam said that his brother wasn't so bad. He was simply trying to find himself. In their private thoughts, Eve and Susan weren't so sure.

<-- 33 -->

Guard Dogs - Beware

"I can't even bring up the subject for fear Adam will go for my throat." Eve's distress was clear.

"Well, she always picks the wrong time," Adam snapped.

"He promises to talk about it later."

"Does he?" Susan queried.

"Of course not! *Later never comes*," Eve practically shouted.

<-- 35 -->

Pleading, Susan turned to Adam. "Seth in our house is ruining our marriage and you act like there's nothing wrong. Don't you care about us?"

<-- 36 -->

Elephant in the Room

Finger Pointing

Adam lashed back insensitively. "My brother's not the problem; you're always nagging and criticizing. That's what's polluting our home!"

Susan asked Eve if she felt that Adam was not considering her viewpoint, and Eve nodded vigorously while Adam looked at the ceiling. "Also, superlatives such as 'always' and 'never' tend to incite defensiveness and counterattack," Susan added.

Unconsciously, Eve clenched her fists.

<-- 39 -->

Bursting out, Eve retaliated, proving Susan's point.

"When will you see what's in front of your nose? Are you the stupidest moron on the planet?"

Susan challenged Eve's verbal assault, pointing out that hurtful name-calling is a dead end.

"Instead of complaints, let's try to work on some solutions," Susan was about to say when Adam had a meltdown.

<-- 40 -->

Pushing Buttons

Toxic Emotions

His face reddened and his body shook, "You know that I hate it when you call me that." Adam's father had often ridiculed him with the nickname '*Moron*.' Worse yet, sometimes Adam secretly feared it was true. He glared at Eve, barely able to contain the toxic shame inserted into him by his father so long ago.

<-- 43 -->

However, Eve, still caught up in the conflict's momentum, ignored him and delivered one final jab. "Adam, with all your visits to Donut Heaven, I should buy stock in the company. We'd be rich! Isn't it time you got off your lazy rear and onto a treadmill?"

Adam retreated, utterly humiliated, and Eve, sensing she had gone too far, became silent and still. Yet, there was a tiny secret part of her that took guilty pleasure in Adam's reaction. It was payback for his refusal to deal with the Seth problem.

<-- 44 -->

Knocked Out

Susan could see that Adam and Eve were suffering from a communication breakdown. Mutual cooperation had turned into destructive power struggles. They had lost the ability to listen and to hear each other. "This must have been painful for you both," Susan summarized. "Next time, we'll work on expressing thoughts and feelings productively and respectfully."

Susan suggested that the couple go out to a movie to redirect their moods. "Enjoy the popcorn." She gave a friendly smile.

<-- 46 -->

Communication Breakdown

Part III

Freedom

I'm not your mother!

The following week, Susan asked Adam what emotions he had been experiencing.

"Angry ... at Eve. You know, I work really hard, but she's always finding something to gripe about."

Eve truly appreciated her husband's devotion to their family, but they had other problems he refused to address. "You just don't get it, and I'm exhausted from explaining to deaf ears."

"Adam," Susan intervened, "did you ever feel this way growing up? Sometimes childhood relationships generate filters that distort our view of the present."

"I'm not sure," Adam mumbled.

<-- 51 -->

Eve, however, *was* sure, declaring, "That mother—some piece of work. Dysfunctional family 101. Adam would come downstairs dressed for school, and she'd send him back up to change his socks that didn't match his pants. *Even if that meant missing his breakfast.* When he got a 98% on a test, she'd ask what happened to the other two points. I could go on ...; all kinds of issues setting everyone on edge. But you couldn't bring them up. Not if you valued your life.

And then, the Dad ..."

<-- 52 -->

Discussion Prohibited

Adam rushed to defend his father. "Eve thinks Dad was too controlling, but he *did* love us. He bragged all the time about his good-looking, talented children."

"Love you!" Eve burst out. "You were his punching bag, and Seth was his golden boy."

<-- 54 -->

Directing Roles

Motive Please!

Eve hammered further. "You can't toss the word love around like salad. Did you ever ask yourself why he *supposedly* 'loved' you? Your talents made *him* look good. He never even recognized, let alone valued, the kind-hearted soul *I* fell in love with."

Susan spoke gently. "Words like 'love' can represent different things to different people. Perhaps Eve is hoping you will question what motivated your father's praise."

<-- 57 -->

Adam was visibly shaken. Hesitantly, he thought back. "It's tough to talk about, but there *were* times when Dad was super-nasty. You couldn't question or disagree with him. Zero tolerance. Even when I was positive he was wrong, I kept my mouth shut. Opposing him would have been suicide."

"Sounds like you were living in an emotional straitjacket," Susan suggested.

"Good way to put it. That's maybe why I'm so connected to Seth. We're the only ones who get how it feels to be on the receiving end of Dad."

"It's understandable that your attachment to Seth helped you to cope. However, perhaps you're not on the same page about everything," Susan proposed.

<-- 58 -->

Invincible Adversary

Eve added, "Why can't you see that your brother is a mirror image of your dad? *It's all about him.* It always has been. Seth doesn't think like you. There are pieces missing, such as a work ethic, fair-mindedness, humility …"

"Adam," Susan suggested, "I'm wondering if you've been taking care of Seth because you're hoping and waiting for him to change."

<-- 60 -->

Cats Don't Bark

Primping the Pig

Eve's pitch raised an octave. "You put those nice clean clothes on Seth's back. Wonderful! Now he *looks* presentable. If it wasn't for you propping him up, he'd still be in that dirty apartment, living on soda and cigarettes. Can't you see that you're the giver and he's the taker?"

<-- 63 -->

Susan could see that Eve's frustration was reaching a critical point.

"How long will you push before you wake up and face the truth? Don't you realize that diapering Seth is getting you nowhere? It's not going to work no matter how hard you try. Meanwhile, our marriage is a shambles!" Eve exploded.

<-- 64 -->

Pushing a Mountain

Outnumbered

Adam shut down from Eve's aggression, and Susan deftly redirected the session. "I think it's time to explore what's truly important to you both at the core." After some reflection, it turned out that the couple had several personal values in common like justice, honesty, respect, and gratitude. "How about your family, Adam, do they share your values?" Susan asked.

Adam exhaled slowly. "I'd rather not admit it, but they aren't the nicest bunch. Like Eve said about my brother, Seth, they tend to be materialistic, self-important, and insensitive. Growing up, I often felt like an alien, but I figured there was something wrong with me."

"The majority isn't always right," Susan countered.

<-- 67 -->

Then, Susan introduced an important concept. "Sometimes we project our personal principles onto others because we unconsciously assume and sincerely desire that they function as we do. Difficult and disappointing as it may be, it makes good sense to discern, respect, and come to accept how others tick."

"You want Seth to act like you, think like you, *care* like you … but he doesn't," Eve concluded.

"It's kind of like … you're a Mac and he's a PC—running different software," Susan suggested.

<-- 68 -->

Projecting

Imminent Revelation

Adam had to admit they were right. Despite valiant attempts at denial, deep inside, he had always known. Turmoil raged in his chest. The long-overdue emergence of this painful truth propelled Adam to the precipice of a breakthrough.

<-- 71 -->

It was Adam's time to choose. Defending his freeloading brother was interfering in his marriage and draining his resources. Bravely, with conviction, he got off the fence. Seth would have to go.

<-- 72 -->

Pick a Side

Disconnect

Humbled and vulnerable, Adam looked toward Susan. "So what now?"

"You ready to take back your power?" Adam nodded. "That's good. Remember when we talked about rewiring yourself? A relationship works the same way. Cord by cord, it's time to sever Seth's control. You can start immediately."

<-- 75 -->

"No" Muscle

Eve suggested that Adam try resisting Seth's regular requests for money.

"Set some limits to protect what is yours. It's time to embrace a powerful word, the word *No*," Susan coached. "Exercise your '*NO*' muscle."

<-- 77 -->

Adam looked perturbed. "But I'll have my head handed to me. Seth can be intimidating like Dad."

"What's the worst that can happen?" Susan asked.

"He'll make me feel guilty and obligated. Like if I don't give him what he wants, he threatens to never speak to me again."

"Imagine that Seth is a child throwing a temper tantrum. Enduring the storm of accusations, emotional appeals, untruths, putdowns, etc. is your process to develop immunity and disarm him. Push aside any impulses to argue and defend. Believe me, when the manipulation toolbox is empty, the winds will die down."

<-- 78 -->

Weather the Storm

Dancing Solo

Eve, having read her share of self-help bestsellers, added in her two cents. "Seth is an emotional blackmailer; you're constantly enabling him and anyway, he's bluffing," she declared.

"So …" Susan began, "it sounds like he's been using your fear of losing him as leverage to get what he wants. A perfect example of a cord that needs disconnecting. Stand your ground and step out of the dance!"

Adam spoke timidly. "But what if he means it?"

"Can you afford *not* to take that risk?" Susan inquired.

<-- 81 -->

Adam stammered, "No," while Susan continued. "Personal growth requires casting off the toxic to make space for healthier experiences. From your position, you are not throwing away your brother. You are offering to renegotiate an equitable relationship contract."

The image of Judas came to mind. He and Seth had things in common, such as prioritizing self-indulgence at any price. *I'm doing my brother a favor by disrupting his comfort zone. As long as Seth can maneuver a handout, he'll never reach for a hand up,* Adam reasoned hopefully.

<-- 82 -->

Throw it Out

Ravaged

Adam reflected on the years of Seth's withdrawals from his bank of resources without any deposits. The relationship had been a one-way street. No wonder he felt so depleted.

<-- 85 -->

Transformed, Adam was glad that reaching his limit had inspired him to seek help. Susan had joined with him, offering empathy, support, and some helpful new tools.

Adam finally recognized that sharing our inborn strengths and talents in the spirit of mutual respect and caring is the circuit of life and love. Don't you agree?

<-- 86 -->

Reciprocity

About the Author

Elizabeth R. Burchard, LSW is a psychotherapist in Northern New Jersey. She holds a BA in Biochemistry from Swarthmore College and an MSW from Fordham University. Elizabeth provides counseling for anxiety, depression, trauma, marital and family challenges, and domestic abuse. She also presents professionally on coercive control in one-on-one, family, and cultic group settings.

CPSIA information can be obtained
at www.ICGtesting.com
Printed in the USA
LVHW061603080120
642937LV00012B/585/P

9 781576 339985